Wild Weather

Blizzard

REVISED AND UPDATED

Catherine Chambers

Heinemann Library
Chicago, Illionis

© 2002, 2007 Heinemann Library
an imprint of Capstone Global Library, LLC
Chicago, Illinois

Customer Service 888-454-2279

Visit our website at www.heinemannraintree.com

Designed by Steve Mead and Q2A Creative
Maps by Paul Bale
Printed in the United States of America in North Mankato, Minnesota. 092012   006924

12
10 9 8 7 6 5 4 3

New edition ISBN: 978-1-403-49575-4 (hardcover)
                    978-1-403-49584-6 (paperback)

The Library of Congress has cataloged the first edition as follows:
Chambers, Catherine, 1954-
Blizzard / Catherine Chambers.
          p. cm. -- (Wild weather)
Summary: Introduces what a blizzard is, and how some humans, plants, and animals have adapted to living in places where these fierce snowstorms are common.
Includes bibliographical references and index.
  ISBN 1-58810-654-3 (HC), 1-4034-0110-1 (Pbk)
  ISBN 978-1-58810-654-4 (HC), 978-1-4034-0110-6 (Pbk)
 1. Blizzards--Juvenile literature. 2. Blizzards – Physiological effect--
Juvenile literature. [1. Blizzards] I. Title. II. Series.
  QC926.37 .C48 2002
  551.55'5--dc21

Acknowledgments

The author and publishers are grateful to the following for permission to reproduce copyright material: Alejandro Alvarez/Philadelphia Daily News/ZUMA Press p15, Associated Press pp17, Blickwinkel/Alamy p24, Corbis pp9, 22, Richard Cummins/SuperStock p14, Digital Vision p7, Ecoscene pp19, 28, Damon Higgins/Palm Beach Post/ZUMA Press p18, Oxford Scientific Films pp5, 6, 16, 23, PA Photos pp4, 11, Papilo pp8, 25, Popperfoto p20, Rex Features p26, Robert Harding Picture Library p27, Stone p12, Stock Market pp21, 29, Topham Picturepoint p13.

Cover photograph of snow falling reproduced with permission of Ryan McVay/Getty Images.

The publishers would like to thank Mark Rogers and the Met Office for their assistance with the preparation of this book.

Some words are shown in bold, **like this**. You can find out what they mean by looking in the glossary.

Contents

What Is a Blizzard?

A blizzard is a very fierce **snowstorm**. It usually happens in winter. Snow falls from the clouds and strong winds blow the snow around.

■ *Snow on streets and sidewalks can make it hard to get places.*

■ *This road has been covered by a snowdrift.*

Wind picks up snow from the ground. The snow is tossed into the air. The wind blows it into deep **drifts**. These snowdrifts cover roads and block doorways.

Where Do Blizzards Happen?

Blizzards often happen on high mountains. This is because the air is colder on high ground. Some mountains are always covered in snow.

■ *Some mountains get a lot of snow.*

North America

Europe

China

Atlantic
Ocean

Pacific
Ocean

Indian
Ocean

Pacific
Ocean

■ *Blizzards
usually happen
in winter.*

Blizzards happen in warmer parts of the world,
too. They happen in North America, northern
Europe and China. In these places they happen
mostly in the cold winter **season**.

What Is Snow?

Snow is made of tiny **crystals** of frozen water. The crystals form high up in the sky. They stick together as they fall. This makes many different snowflake shapes and patterns.

■ *Every snowflake crystal has a different pattern.*

■ *Skiing is a fun sport to do in the snow.*

Snow falls in layers. Some snow is dry and powdery. This is good for skiing. Other snow is wet and heavy. This is better for making snowballs!

Why Do Blizzards Happen?

Blizzards happen when **crystals** of frozen water form in clouds. The crystals get so heavy that they stick together and fall as snow. They whirl down from the clouds, making a **snowstorm**.

Cloud

Snow

■ *Snowflakes fall from a cloud to make a snowstorm.*

■ *A blizzard can make a walk very difficult.*

Sometimes a cold wave of air rushes in behind the snowstorm. These freezing winds blow the snow all around. When snow is blown by strong winds the storm is called a blizzard.

11

What Are Blizzards Like?

Blizzard winds make the air icy cold. The thick snow makes it hard to see ahead. Then the snow settles into big **drifts**.

■ *Big piles of snow can take a long time to melt.*

■ *Blizzards can make driving difficult and dangerous.*

It is dangerous to drive through a blizzard. The snowflakes stop the driver from seeing the road. The road gets slippery with the icy snow.

Blizzard in the City

The city of Philadelphia is in southeastern Pennsylvania. In the winter of 2005 the city was hit by a strong blizzard.

■ *Philadelphia can be warm in the summer.*

■ *It was difficult to travel in the blizzards of 2005.*

The streets were blocked with snow. Airplanes had to stay on the ground. Cars were covered in snow.

Harmful Blizzards

Blizzards can stop people from reaching hospitals and schools. Trucks cannot deliver food to grocery stores.

■ *This car is completely covered in snow.*

Blizzards make thick layers of snow on the mountains. Sometimes these layers slip. Then an **avalanche** of snow tumbles down. It can bury people and animals.

Preparing for Blizzards

Weather forecasts can often tell when a blizzard is coming. The weather forecasters give out weather warnings. Then people can prepare for the blizzard.

■ *Computers help us keep track of the weather.*

■ *Snow cannot settle if salt is spread on the road.*

Roads can be prepared for a blizzard. Road workers spread special salt on the roads. This melts the snow as it falls on the road.

How Do People Cope With Blizzards?

Snowplows are used to clear roads during and after blizzards. They have big shovels that push snow into piles at the side of the road.

■ *This snowplow is clearing a road so cars can get through.*

■ *It is important to dress very warmly in a blizzard.*

People wear heavy coats to protect them from blizzard winds. Hats, scarves, and mittens are also important for keeping warm. Boots keep people safe and dry in the snow.

Coping With Blizzards—Inuit

This boy is an Inuit. Inuit are people who live in the cold **Arctic region**. This boy wears layers of clothing that trap warm air. He has a fur-lined hood and snow boots to protect him from the cold.

■ *This boy's clothes keep him warm even when it is very cold.*

■ *These men are building an igloo.*

Some Inuit can build houses quickly out
of blocks of snow. This protects them from
blizzards. Inuit can catch fish by making holes
in the thick ice and snow that cover the sea.

How Does Nature Cope?

Lambs are sometimes born under the snow during a blizzard. The mother's body melts the snow around it. This makes a warm space to keep the lamb alive.

■ *Sheep have thick woolly coats to keep them warm during blizzards.*

■ *These flowers can grow on cold mountains.*

This mountain flower has hairy leaves. They let in light but protect the plant from blizzard winds. Many plants die in winter. Their roots or seeds lie safe underground.

To the Rescue!

In the mountains, trained dogs can sniff out people buried by **avalanches.** Rescuers follow the dogs. Then the rescuers push long poles into the snow to find the people.

■ *Rescuers dig for people trapped in the snow.*

■ *This car has skidded off the road in the snow.*

People have to be very careful if they are driving through a blizzard. Sometimes there are accidents and rescue services have to pull cars out of the snow.

Adapting to Blizzards

The big, slanted roofs of these houses protect people inside from the snow. The snow falls away from doors and walls.

■ *In the winter, these houses may be covered in snow.*

■ *It is important to shelter somewhere warm in a blizzard.*

Snow lodges like this one are often built in wild mountain forests. Walkers can shelter inside when there is a blizzard. They can find food and make a warm fire.

Fact File

◆ The northeast **coast** of the United States gets very bad blizzards. On February 12, 2006, 27 inches (69 centimeters) of snow fell in New York in just a few hours. Thousands of people were stranded at airports.

◆ Strong blizzard winds can blow snow on the ground into snowballs. These are called "snow rollers."

Glossary

Arctic region area around the North Pole. The area around the South Pole is called the Antarctic region.

avalanche when a thick, heavy layer of snow slips down a mountainside

coast strip of land next to a large body of water

crystal shape that is formed when water freezes

drift snow that is blown into a thick mound

season months of the year that have the same type of weather

snow lodge building that shelters walkers in a blizzard

snowplow vehicle that can clear the snow from roads

snowstorm heavy snow and strong winds brought by large dark clouds

weather forecast information predicting the weather that we will get in the future

More Books to Read

Jennings, Terry. *The Weather: Snow*. Mankato, Minn.: Chrysalis Children's Books, 2004

Mayer, Cassie. *Weather Watchers: Snow*. Chicago: Heinemann Library, 2006

Index